THE LIBRARY OF HIP-HOP BIOGRAPHIES™

Kanye West

Laura La Bella

ROSEN PUBLISHING
New York

For Kris and Alicia, the only couple I know who played "Gold Digger" at their wedding

Published in 2009 by The Rosen Publishing Group, Inc.
29 East 21st Street, New York, NY 10010

Copyright © 2009 by The Rosen Publishing Group, Inc.

First Edition

All rights reserved. No part of this book may be reproduced in any form without permission in writing from the publisher, except by a reviewer.

Library of Congress Cataloging-in-Publication Data

La Bella, Laura.
 Kanye West / Laura La Bella.—1st ed.
    p. cm.—(The library of hip-hop biographies)
 Includes bibliographical references, discography, and index.
 ISBN-13: 978-1-4358-5053-8 (library binding)
 ISBN-13: 978-1-4358-5439-0 (pbk)
 ISBN-13: 978-1-4358-5445-1 (6 pack)
 1. West, Kanye—Juvenile literature. 2. Rap musicians—United States—Biography—Juvenile literature. I. Title.
 ML3930.W42L3 2009
 782.421649092—dc22
 [B]
                                                              2008026346

Manufactured in the United States of America

CPSIA Compliance Information: Batch #CG115130YA: For Further Information Contact Rosen Publishing, New York, New York at 1-800-237-9932.

On the cover: Kanye West performs at the Los Angeles Coliseum as part of a concert celebrating the NFL Opening Kickoff celebration, the National Football League's festivities preceding the first game of the new football season.

CONTENTS

INTRODUCTION		**4**
CHAPTER ONE	Raising Kanye	**6**
CHAPTER TWO	A Turning Point Leads to Smash Success	**15**
CHAPTER THREE	Can't Stop the Beat	**23**
CHAPTER FOUR	Courting Controversy	**31**
TIMELINE		**40**
DISCOGRAPHY		**42**
GLOSSARY		**42**
FOR MORE INFORMATION		**44**
FOR FURTHER READING		**45**
BIBLIOGRAPHY		**45**
INDEX		**47**

INTRODUCTION

In 2001, Kanye West burst onto the hip-hop scene as a hitmaker. He produced songs for some of today's biggest artists in R & B, hip-hop, and rap, including superstars like Jay-Z, Alicia Keys, and Common. But while he excelled at creating music for others, his real passion was to be a rapper, not to produce hits for everyone else. He would work hard to persuade the executives at Roc-A-Fella Records to take a chance on him. He would find inspiration for his music in the most unlikely of places, such as an accident that almost took his life. He would transform his rapid-fire thoughts into lyrics and launch an impressive music career fueled by the stellar success of his first album, *The College Dropout*. The unlikely rapper with the designer clothing and middle-class upbringing continued to beat the odds and watch his success grow with the release of more albums. His second album, *Late Registration*, sold an impressive 860,000 copies in its first week. *Graduation*, his third album, sold a stunning 957,000 copies in its first week, even though it was pitted against rapper 50 Cent's newest release. With each new album, West seems to grow larger than life as he touches a chord in fans who keep coming back for more of his powerful lyrics and killer beats.

But there is more to West than his music. He has become a force at awards shows, not just for his theatrical videos and stage performances, but for his outspoken attempts to fight against injustices, big and small. Throughout his music career, he has never stopped creating hits for other artists, even as his own recording career took off. And when his mother, with whom he had forged an unbreakable bond, died unexpectedly, West slowed down just long enough to reevaluate where he was in his life and consider the many lessons his mother taught him about success.

As he launches new albums and world tours and continues to churn out hits for other artists, there seems to be no stopping the hit machine that is Kanye West.

CHAPTER ONE
RAISING KANYE

When Kanye West approached the executives at Roc-A-Fella Records in 2002 about stepping out from his role as a producer and into that of an artist, there was a long moment of hesitation. As a producer, West had created hit songs for Roc-A-Fella's three biggest artists: Jay-Z, Cam'ron, and Beanie Sigel. He had earned a reputation for having a great ear for music and a dedicated work ethic. But emerging from behind the scenes to become an artist was a long shot.

Damon Dash, then the CEO of Roc-A-Fella Records, was the first to recognize Kanye West's talent as a producer. He hired West, who produced hits for a number of artists before he stepped behind the mic himself.

West did not fit the role of a traditional rapper. "Kanye wore a pink shirt with the collar sticking up and Gucci loafers," Damon Dash, then the CEO of Roc-A-Fella, told *Time* magazine. Dash clearly thought West didn't fit into the image of what a rap artist should be. Shawn "Jay-Z" Carter, one of the most successful rappers of all time with more than fifty million records sold and a former CEO of both Def Jam Recordings and Roc-A-Fella Records, agreed with Dash. In the same interview, Jay-Z shared his thoughts on the difference between other artists and Kanye. "We all grew up street guys who had to do whatever we had to do to get by. Then there's Kanye, who to my knowledge has never hustled a day in his life."

A SUBURBAN CHILDHOOD

It's true that Kanye West did not have to "hustle" to get by when he was growing up. In fact, his upbringing was the polar opposite of those artists he has produced. West was raised in a middle-class neighborhood in Chicago, Illinois.

Born on June 8, 1977, in Atlanta, Georgia, West's parents were successful, highly educated professionals who worked hard and taught their son that education, ambition, and determination were the keys to success. His mother, Donda West, earned a master's degree in English from Atlanta University and a doctorate in English education at Auburn University. His father, Ray West, worked as a photojournalist for the *Atlanta-Journal Constitution*, one of the most prestigious newspapers in the United States. Not only was Ray West one of the first black photojournalists for the paper, but he was also an award-winning photographer. In addition, Kanye West's father was active in the civil rights movement of the 1960s as a member of the Black Panthers, a militant African American organization that forcefully raised awareness of "black power" and promoted civil rights in the United States.

As an only child, West lived in Atlanta until his parents divorced when he was three years old. He then moved to Chicago with his mother, who accepted a teaching position with Chicago State University, where she would eventually become the chair of the school's English department. Even though he was separated from his father, West spent every summer back in Atlanta with him. When his mother's job took her to Nanjing, China, where she was offered a visiting professorship at a local university, West went with her and spent a year there.

EARLY MUSICAL INFLUENCES

While Jay-Z dropped out of high school and Cam'ron and Sigel had their share of legal troubles in their youth and early adulthood, West's life was significantly less dramatic. He was raised in a suburban neighborhood where he attended good schools. His mother insisted that he take classical music and art lessons.

Like many other teens growing up in the 1980s, West was discovering a new, edgy sound in music: rap and hip-hop. He liked what he heard, particularly from Run-D.M.C., a pioneering hip-hop group. His other major musical influence was the biggest musical artist in the world in the '80s: Michael Jackson, the former boy wonder who fronted the Jackson 5 (a band composed of Michael and four of his older brothers) before going solo. Both Run-D.M.C. and Jackson would prove to have an immediate and lasting effect upon West.

West and his mother, Donda West, celebrate the release of her book *Raising Kanye: Life Lessons from the Mother of a Hip-Hop Superstar.*

Run-D.M.C. was founded by Joseph "Run" Simmons, Darryl "D.M.C." McDaniels, and Jason "Jam-Master Jay" Mizell. All three men grew up in Queens, New York, and rhymed about everything from materialism to higher education, topics to which West could relate. The group is widely credited with introducing the hip-hop style of music into the mainstream. Run-D.M.C. was the first rap group to have a number one R & B rap album, the first to appear on the cover of *Rolling Stone* magazine, and the first ever to earn a Grammy nomination.

Michael Jackson was the biggest pop star in the world in the 1980s. When his second solo album, *Thriller*, was released in 1982, West was just five years old. *Thriller* went on to become one of the world's best-selling albums of all time. The singer made a powerful impression on West. In an interview with *Spin* magazine, West talked about the influence Jackson's music, performances, and style had on his life. "Michael Jackson is my favorite artist of all time. Every time I hit the stage, every time I write a song, every time I write a rap, every performance I do, every time I pick out an outfit, I think about Michael Jackson. Michael Jackson is synonymous with the greatest that you could possibly do in music," he said.

The *Thriller* album, fueled by hits like "Billie Jean," "Beat It," and "Wanna Be Startin' Somethin'," remained in the top ten on the Billboard 200 chart for a full year and went on to sell

Among West's musical influences is Michael Jackson, one of the biggest musical artists in history. Jackson's album *Thriller* is the best-selling album of all time.

a stunning twenty-seven million copies that year. In the end, it spent eighty consecutive weeks on the chart, and thirty-seven weeks in the number-one position. Remarkably, even today, the album still sells more than 130,000 copies in the United States every year. It holds a place in the *Guinness Book of World Records* as the world's best-selling album of all time. As of 2007, the album has sold a reported sixty-five million copies worldwide.

FOLLOWING THE BEAT OF HIS OWN DRUM

For West, who began making beats when he was fourteen years old, Run-D.M.C. and Jackson represented the height of success

ROC-A-FELLA RECORDS

Jay-Z and his then-business partners Damon Dash and Kareem "Biggs" Burke needed a way to put out Jay-Z's music. With no luck signing a record deal with any of the major labels, the three decided to establish one of their own dedicated to rap and hip-hop music. They founded Roc-A-Fella Records in 1996. The label's name is a reference to American oil magnate and multimillionaire businessman John Rockefeller. Roc-A-Fella's artists include Jay-Z, Kanye West, Common, and Beanie Sigel.

RAISING KANYE

in music, the standard by which West would measure himself. He started saving his ten-dollar-a-week allowance to purchase an eight-bit sampler, and he began to play around, looking for a sound to call his own.

As West neared the end of his high school years at Polaris High School in suburban Oak Lawn, Illinois, he knew he wanted to be a rapper. But his parents had other ideas. They wanted him to go to college and get an education." My plan was that he would get at least one degree, if not several," his mother told *Time* magazine in an interview. To please his mother, West enrolled in art school and took classes at Chicago State University. But his main interest remained music. He finally confronted his parents with his ambition to become a rap artist. After months of convincing them that he could make a living, his parents finally gave in. Donda West told her son that he could take one year off from school to pursue rapping and producing.

Kanye West appears at Chicago State University for MTVu Stand In, a program that brings cultural icons into a classroom. While there, West taught a master class in songwriting.

13

With the drive and ambition his parents instilled in him, West jumped at the chance to start his music career. During the day, he worked as a telemarketer to pay two hundred dollars a month in rent to his mother, which she demanded from him during his year off from school. At night, he worked on his music and his sound, while also making beats for other rappers. Within a few months, a Chicago-area rapper bought a beat that West had created, thereby officially launching the start of his professional career. "That's when I knew the one-year plan was out the window," his mother told *Time* magazine. It wasn't too long before he caught the attention of executives at Roc-A-Fella Records, where he started producing music for other artists.

CHAPTER TWO
A TURNING POINT LEADS TO SMASH SUCCESS

Kanye West's unique beats were catchy and attention grabbing. Soon after selling his first beat, West found himself becoming the hotshot producer to some of the biggest artists in hip-hop and rap. He signed a contract to work with Roc-A-Fella Records and began producing songs for Jermaine Dupri, a producer and rapper, and Foxy Brown, a highly successful female rapper.

West's really big break, however, was when his work appeared on Jay-Z's 2001 album, *The Blueprint*.

Featured heavily, West produced four of the album's thirteen tracks, which helped to cement West as a major name in hip-hop production. After *The Blueprint* was released, West found himself producing hits for Ludacris ("Stand Up") and Alicia Keys ("You Don't Know My Name").

TRYING TO BREAK THE MOLD

In 2002, Jay-Z released *The Blueprint 2: The Gift & the Curse*, which featured West rapping on the single, "The Bounce." At the time West was not yet an artist, but he was an accomplished producer, having racked up a number of hits for other artists. But what West really wanted to do was release his own album and become a rapper. He found himself determined to get a record deal, but not everyone thought West had what it took to succeed, including his friend and mentor Jay-Z. The rapper was among those who were reluctant to support West's future career. Jay-Z saw West as a producer, not a performer.

West struggled to find a record company that would sign him. Roc-A-Fella, with whom he had produced big hits, passed

Kanye West and Roc-A-Fella Records founder Jay-Z appear together at the MTV Video Music Awards. Jay-Z initially passed on signing West to a record deal but later changed his mind.

on him, as did other record labels both large and small. They all seemed to struggle with the idea that a rapper who looked like West could have an edge to him. Each record company turned him down with the same message: He was not the

KANYE WEST: HITMAKER TO THE STARS

Some of the hit albums Kanye West had a hand in producing include:

Foxy Brown, *Chyna Doll* (1998)
Goodie Mob, *World Party* (1999)
Beanie Sigel, *The Truth* (2000)
Lil' Kim, *The Notorious K.I.M.* (2000)
Jay-Z, *The Dynasty: Roc La Familia* (2000)
Beanie Sigel, *The Reason* (2001)
Jay-Z, *The Blueprint* (2001)
Cam'ron, *Come Home with Me* (2002)
Nas, *The Lost Tapes* (2002)
Jay-Z, *The Blueprint 2: The Gift & the Curse* (2002)
Talib Kweli, *Quality* (2002)
Fabolous, *Street Dreams* (2003)
Cam'ron, *Cam'ron Presents . . . The Diplomats—Diplomatic Immunity* (2003)
Lil' Kim, *La Bella Mafia* (2003)
Beyoncé, *Dangerously in Love* (2003)
DMX, *Grand Champ* (2003)
Ludacris, *Chicken-N-Beer* (2003)
Jay-Z, *The Black Album* (2003)
Alicia Keys, *The Diary of Alicia Keys* (2003)
Twista, *Kamikaze* (2004)
Janet Jackson, *Damita Jo* (2004)
Jadakiss, *Kiss of Death* (2004)
Brandy, *Afrodisiac* (2004)
Mobb Deep, *Amerikaz Nightmare* (2004)
Shyne, *Godfather Buried Alive* (2004)
Talib Kweli, *The Beautiful Struggle* (2004)
Mos Def, *The New Danger* (2004)
Cam'ron, *Purple Haze* (2004)
John Legend, *Get Lifted* (2004)
Mariah Carey, *The Emancipation of Mimi* (2005)
Keyshia Cole, *The Way It Is* (2005)
Diddy, *Press Play* (2006)
John Legend, *Once Again* (2006)
Jay-Z, *Kingdom Come* (2006)
Nas, *Hip-Hop Is Dead* (2006)
Talib Kweli, *Eardrum* (2007)
Michael Jackson, *Thriller 25* (2008)

A TURNING POINT LEADS TO SMASH SUCCESS

stereotypical artist with the street image that was prominent in the hip-hop culture.

To an extent, West agreed with them. "It was a strike against me that I didn't wear baggy jeans and jerseys and that I never hustled, never sold drugs," West told *Time* magazine in an interview about his struggles to find a place in hip-hop music. But as a producer, he knew what music would sell, and he was sure that if he could get a record deal, he would succeed. "I can't tell you how frustrating it was that they didn't get that," he said in that same interview.

A NEW LIFE AFTER NEAR DEATH

Roc-A-Fella Records finally came around and gave him a recording contract. West threw himself into his music. He spent most of his time, sometimes well into the night, writing and producing music for his debut album. In the meantime, he continued to produce music for other artists.

It was an exhausting effort on West's part, one that almost cost him his life. In the early-morning hours on October 23, 2002, he was driving home from the recording studio when he fell asleep at the wheel of his car and crashed. The accident was nearly fatal. Among West's extensive injuries was a jaw broken in three places. He required emergency surgery. West spent nearly two weeks in the hospital recovering before going home to continue a lengthy recuperation. His jaw would end up being wired shut for several weeks while it healed from the accident.

19

KANYE WEST

While recovering in the hospital after a car accident, Kanye West heard Chaka Khan's *(above)* hit "Through the Fire." West soon penned his own song, "Through the Wire," in which he sampled Khan's beats.

The car accident had a huge impact on West's life. "The accident changed my focus," he told *Rolling Stone* magazine. While he was in the hospital recovering, he heard Chaka Khan's hit song "Through the Fire." Khan was a Grammy Award–winning singer whose musical style combined hip-hop, jazz, and R & B. As West listened to the song, the lyrics inspired him to write "Through the Wire," a song about his car accident. "He called me from his hospital bed with his jaw wired shut and asked for a drum machine," says Damon Dash. "That impressed me."

Just a few days after leaving the hospital, and only two weeks after the accident, West went to a studio and recorded "Through the Wire." His jaw was still wired, and he mumbled through most of the lyrics. He used the beats from Khan's song in the background. The resulting single finally persuaded Roc-A-Fella to move ahead with West's full-length album. "Death is the best

A TURNING POINT LEADS TO SMASH SUCCESS

thing that can ever happen to a rapper," West told *Time* magazine. "Almost dying isn't bad either." The song later became the lead single for his debut album, *The College Dropout*.

After the car accident, West approached his music career with more intensity and a renewed dedication and ambition. While he recovered from the accident, his album was delayed to give him time to heal. He continued to work on producing hits for other artists, among them Talib Kweli ("Get By"), Jay-Z and Beyoncé ("'03 Bonnie & Clyde"), and Twista ("Slow Jamz"), which featured a collaboration between Twista, West, and comedian and actor Jamie Foxx. West and Foxx, a multitalented Academy Award–winning actor who had his own debut album in the works, added extra verses to the song. When it was released, it quickly climbed the charts and became a number-one hit. The song added much interest and anticipation to West's debut album.

A FIRST-TIME SENSATION

In 2004, West's album finally debuted. *The College Dropout* became a huge commercial and critical success. The album sold 441,000 copies in its first week—an extraordinary number for a debut album—and more than three million copies overall. It topped all the major critics' polls and earned ten Grammy nominations.

Perhaps more important, West's album created a fresh and angst-ridden portrait of the African American middle class, a segment of the population that does not get much attention. It also

The College Dropout, Kanye West's debut album, sold 441,000 copies in its first week. West went out on tour to support the album.

made rap music accessible to audiences that hadn't paid attention in years and revitalized hip-hop. Jamie Foxx told *Time* magazine that the album "restored my faith in hip-hop." Jay-Z, who was skeptical about whether West could be successful, also offered his congratulations. "It makes me proud as someone who's watched his growth from the beginning, when he came in as a hungry producer, to now he's a rock star. I'm happy for him on that level," he told *Entertainment Weekly*.

One of the greatest compliments West received about the album came from one of his idols, Darryl McDaniels of Run-D.M.C. McDaniels told *Time* magazine that he had stopped listening to hip-hop altogether. "This past decade, it seems like hip-hop has mostly been about parties and guns and women. That's fine if you're in a club, but from 9 AM till I went to bed at night, the music had nothing to say to me." What did speak to him was West's song, "Jesus Walks." "When I heard it, I just stopped in my tracks," McDaniels said.

CHAPTER THREE
CAN'T STOP THE BEAT

With a number-one album and critical acclaim, Kanye West proved that if he was a hip-hop contradiction — a middle-class, suburban rapper — then hip-hop itself was rife with contradiction and complexity. The album was expertly produced, but what made it compelling to its audience was the way the songs challenged listeners. On "Jesus Walks," there was a mix of spirituality and doubt. It was a rap song but also featured a gospel choir singing backup.

KANYE WEST

Kanye West and *The College Dropout* were nominated for nine Grammy Awards. West walked away with three, including Best Rap Album.

Throughout the whole album, West's lyrics were simple yet complex. They came off as both smart and dopey, arrogant and insecure. On *The College Dropout*, West found a way to produce amazing rap music that avoided the violence and self-destruction that other artists weaved throughout their music. Damon Dash summed it up to *Time* magazine by saying West "combines the superficialness that the urban demographic needs with conscious rhymes for the kids with backpacks."

The album featured guest appearances by artists for whom West had produced music. These included Jay-Z, Ludacris, GLC, Consequence, Talib Kweli, Mos Def, Common, and Syleena Johnson. When the 2005 Grammy nominations came out, West was nominated for nine awards, including Album of the Year and Best Rap Album for *The College Dropout*, Song of the Year and Best Rap Song for "Jesus Walks," Best Rap Solo Performance for "Through the Wire," and Best New Artist. West went on to win three Grammys.

CAN'T STOP THE BEAT

AND THE WINNER IS . . . .

Kanye West has received more than one hundred nominations for his work as an artist and producer. This is just a sampling of the awards he has won.

2004   BET Award, Best New Artist

2005   Grammy Award, Best R & B Song "You Don't Know My Name"
            (producing honor)
        Grammy Award, Best Rap Song, "Jesus Walks"
        Grammy Award, Best Rap Album, *The College Dropout*
        MTV Europe Music Awards, Best Hip-Hop Act
        MTV Music Video Awards, Best Male Video, "Jesus Walks"
        Vibe Awards, Best Rapper

2006   Grammy Award, Best Rap Solo Performance, "Gold Digger"
        Grammy Award, Best Rap Song, "Diamonds from Sierra Leone"
        Grammy Award, Best Rap Album, *Late Registration*
        Billboard R & B/Hip-Hop Awards, Top Rap Album, *Late Registration*
        Billboard R & B/Hip-Hop Awards, Hot Rap Track of the Year, "Gold Digger"
        Billboard R & B/Hip-Hop Awards, Top R & B/Hip-Hop Album Artist

2008   Grammy Award, Best Rap Solo Performance, "Stronger"
        Grammy Award, Best Rap Performance (Duo or Group), "Southside"
        Grammy Award, Best Rap Song, "Good Life"
        Grammy Award, Best Rap Album, *Graduation*

THE SOPHOMORE EFFORT

West returned to the studio and began work on his second album, *Late Registration*. In a review, *Rolling Stone* magazine called the album "an undeniable triumph, packed front to back, so expansive it makes [West's] debut [album] sound like a rough draft." West's second album sold more than 860,000 copies in the first week it was released.

Kanye West appears at Tower Records in New York to celebrate the release of his second album, *Late Registration*. First week sales of 860,000 units were more than double those of his first album.

Late Registration had a series of four hit singles: "Diamonds from Sierra Leone," "Touch the Sky," "Heard 'Em Say," and the album's biggest hit, "Gold Digger," which featured Jamie Foxx performing background vocals. At the time of the "Gold Digger" release, it broke a record for the most digital downloads in a week, selling more than eighty thousand units. It was also the fastest-selling digital download to date. One song on the album that was especially touching was "Hey Mama," which was dedicated to West's mother, with whom he had always been extremely close.

DOING IT ALL

Late Registration went on to earn eight Grammy Award nominations. At the ceremony in 2006, West won three: Best Rap Solo Performance for "Gold Digger," Best Rap Song for "Diamonds from Sierra Leone," and Best Rap Album.

As West released his second album, he never strayed far from producing music for other artists. He continued to churn out hits for Twista ("Overnight Celebrity"), Janet Jackson ("I Want You"), Brandy ("Talk About Our Love"), the Game ("Dreams"), Common ("Go!"), and Keyshia Cole ("I Changed My Mind").

With such success as an artist and a producer, West soon established his own record label. He calls it GOOD Music, which stands for "Getting Out Our Dreams." His record label released an album by John Legend, titled *Get Lifted*, and then released an album by Common called *Be*. Yet, even though he had added more job titles to his name—rapper, producer, and record executive—West continued to record his own music. He soon released his third album, *Graduation*.

RAP RELEASE RIVALRY

In the weeks leading up to the album's release, a rivalry began between West and 50 Cent, a rapper who rose to fame with the

KANYE WEST

As he prepares to launch his third album, Kanye West and rapper 50 Cent get into a war of words. *Graduation* sold 957,000 units in its first week, easily outselling 50 Cent's album.

release of his first two albums, *Get Rich or Die Tryin'* and *The Massacre*. Both albums sold more than twenty-one million copies combined. The rapper and West had albums scheduled to be released on the same day, September 11, 2007.

Fueled by 50 Cent's comments that West's success was entirely owed to him, West challenged the rapper to a showdown. 50 Cent responded by declaring that he would retire if West's album sold more copies than his own. To *Rolling Stone* magazine,

50 Cent said, "I'm King Kong. Kanye is human. Humans run when they see King Kong, because they're scared."

50 Cent took the challenge a step further, saying he'd be willing to debate West on live television on the question of whose album was better. West dismissed 50 Cent's comments and focused instead on the music. Taking the high road, he stated to *Rolling Stone*, "When I heard that thing about the debate, I thought that was the stupidest thing. When my album drops and 50's album drops, you're gonna get a lot of good music at the same time." Unable to let the feud die, 50 Cent then predicted that the release date of West's album would change, claiming that Jay-Z, the head of West's record label, would cave under the competitive pressure. Jay-Z didn't. Instead, he issued comments saying he'd welcome the head-to-head competition.

On September 11, 2007, both albums were released, and it quickly became apparent that West's *Graduation* would outsell *Curtis*, 50 Cent's album. *Graduation* sold 957,000 copies in its first week. By contrast, *Curtis* sold 691,000 copies. The rivalry led to outstanding sales of both albums. In fact, it marked only the second time since Nielsen SoundScan began collecting data in 1991 that two albums sold more than 600,000 copies in the same week in the United States. *Graduation* topped the charts all over the world, including number-one positions in Canada, England, Australia, Austria, Belgium, and the Billboard European Top 100 albums. In an album review, *Rolling Stone* said, "This is an album that you first like, then love."

Kanye West celebrates the release of his third album, *Graduation*, at Virgin Megastore in New York, where he signs autographs and meets fans.

Graduation went on to earn eight Grammy nominations. West would win four, for Best Rap Solo Performance for the song "Stronger," Best Rap Performance by a Duo or Group for the song "Southside," Best Rap Song for "Good Life," and Best Rap Album.

Since the release of his first album, West has become a highly decorated artist and producer. He has earned more than one hundred nominations from the Grammys, Billboard Awards, MTV Video Music Awards, Teen Choice Awards, Vibe Awards, and the World Music Awards. West has taken home more than thirty trophies for both his own albums and his producing work on those of other artists.

CHAPTER FOUR
COURTING CONTROVERSY

Kanye West's three albums have sold millions of copies to date. He's crafted hit songs for some of today's biggest artists. But West has become known just as much for his very public and attention-getting vocal outbursts as he has for his hitmaking abilities. He has endured a fair amount of controversy for statements he's made over the past several years. But West is nothing if not outspoken.

KANYE WEST

AWARD SHOW MELTDOWNS

West first became known for his perceived arrogance when he made comments after the 2006 Grammy nominations were announced. He told MTV News that he would "really have a problem" if he didn't win for Album of the Year. "I don't care what I do, I don't care how much I stunt—you can never take away from the amount of work I put into it." West did not win the award.

West's controversial behavior continued on November 2, 2006, when his video for the single "Touch the Sky" failed to win the Best Video Award at the MTV Europe Music Awards. When the award's winners were announced, West stepped on to the stage. As the award was being presented to Justice and Simian for their single, "We Are Your Friends," West argued onstage that he should have won the award instead. After the awards ceremony ended, news outlets around the world reported

Kanye West, having lost the Best Video Award at the MTV Europe Music Awards to Justice and Simian, jumped onstage to say he should have won.

COURTING CONTROVERSY

on his behavior. Less than a week later, during a concert performance in Australia on November 7, 2006, he apologized for interrupting the award presentation and for his comments.

Yet, West's behavior at award shows continued in this manner each time another artist was selected as a winner over him. In addition to suggesting that award shows are fixed when he doesn't win, he has stormed out of the audience on a number of occasions and has criticized other artists for winning. Possibly the most public of his outbursts occurred at the 2007 MTV Video Music Awards. West was upset when he performed in a suite at the Palms Hotel and Casino in Las Vegas, the site of the show, instead of on the main stage, like several others acts. He was captured on tape while standing backstage. In an expletive-filled rant, he swore he'd never return to MTV again. In an article on MTV.com, sources suggested that West was also upset that, though nominated in five categories, he took no awards home.

The next day, West appeared as a guest on New York's Z100 radio station. In the interview, he said he felt betrayed by MTV and repeated his vow not to work with the network again. "I wasn't mad that I just didn't win any awards," he said on-air. "For me, MTV made it seem like performing on the main stage was a bad thing, and the suites were just so great. It was my dream when I made 'Stronger' to open up the VMAs with a real power performance."

Within days, an MTV representative issued a statement saying, "[To say that] MTV does not wish to work with him would be

inaccurate. . . . He has been the one who has been vocal about saying he will never work with us again."

GOING OFF THE SCRIPT

Perhaps Kanye West's most controversial and notorious moment in the spotlight, however, came during the Hurricane Katrina Telethon in September 2005. This was an event designed to raise money for the victims of the cataclysmic hurricane that flooded New Orleans, Louisiana, and devastated areas of the Gulf Coast. The rapper was among the many celebrities who donated their time to participate in the telethon, which channeled its proceeds into the American Red Cross Disaster Relief Fund. The one-hour special was produced by NBC News and televised on the NBC network, as well as NBC's cable networks MSNBC and CNBC. It featured performances and appearances by actors, actresses, singers, and various other celebrities.

West and actor and comedian Mike Myers were paired together and scheduled to appear in a short segment about halfway through the show. The two were supposed to take turns reading a prepared script describing the breach in the levees around New Orleans that led to flooding. West decided not to follow the prepared script and instead spoke freely about how he felt the U.S. government was failing miserably in its response to the devastation in Louisiana and Mississippi. His live, unscripted rant included a staunch criticism of President George W. Bush,

COURTING CONTROVERSY

During a telethon for the victims of Hurricane Katrina, Kanye West departed from the prepared script that he and Mike Myers were given and instead criticized the U.S. government's disaster-relief efforts.

calling into question Bush's level of concern and compassion for African Americans.

NBC Universal, the company that owns the NBC network, MSNBC, and CNBC, quickly issued a statement after the broadcast. It read, "Kanye West departed from the scripted comments that were prepared for him, and his opinions in no way represent the views of the networks. It would be most unfortunate if the efforts of the artists who participated tonight and the generosity of millions of Americans who are helping those in need are overshadowed by one person's opinion." Because of the three-hour time difference between the East and West coasts, NBC had time to edit out West's comments before airing the program for West Coast viewers. But millions of people witnessed West's comments nevertheless, and many more read or heard about them later.

A MOTHER'S LOVE, INFLUENCE, AND LOSS

West's passion for speaking his mind comes from his mother, who taught him to "speak his mind and to tell the truth." In an interview with *Jet* magazine to promote her book, *Raising Kanye*, Donda West commented on her son's televised outburst, saying that she trained her son for greatness. "There is no room for shyness. I raised him that way, to think critically and analytically and not be afraid to voice what you feel. I helped shape that. I think leaders are people who must do that."

Teaching her son to speak his mind was not her only influence on him. She also taught West to give back to the community. Together, the mother-son team cofounded the Kanye West Foundation. Established in 2003, the foundation aims to combat the dropout rate in high schools across the United States by developing student-centered programs geared toward increased literacy, heightened self-worth, independent thinking, and self-actualization through the arts. The signature initiative of the foundation is Loop Dreams. Designed to capitalize upon students'

COURTING CONTROVERSY

interest in hip-hop, Loop Dreams challenges students to learn more about what's behind the hip-hop culture in order to help them develop skills, express themselves creatively, and be empowered. West holds benefit concerts to raise money for the foundation so it can support its initiatives around the country.

Unfortunately, Donda West would not live long enough to see the long-term impact of the foundation. On November 10, 2007, she died unexpectedly following cosmetic surgery. It was a devastating loss for Kanye.

West established the Kanye West Foundation, whose mascot is the Dropout Bear, in order to raise money to help reduce high school dropout rates.

West posted a message on his Web log saying he had been putting his priorities in place since his mother's death. "If there's anything my mom taught me, [it] is to enjoy life. I don't do anything I don't love anymore . . . While people chase money, I pursue happiness."

Donda West's funeral was held in her hometown of Oklahoma City, Oklahoma, on November 20, 2007. West held his first concert two days later, on November 22, at the O2, a club in

37

London, England. He dedicated a performance of "Hey Mama" to his mother. The tribute song appears on his second album, *Late Registration*. West launched his *Glow in the Dark* tour shortly after the funeral. At every concert stop, he sang "Hey Mama" and dedicated the performance to his mother. West also performed the song at the Grammy Awards in 2007.

A COURAGEOUS STANCE

West has long been outspoken against homophobia in the supermacho and aggressively heterosexual hip-hop community. It's a topic that very few rap and hip-hop artists will even talk about, let alone stand behind. During an interview with MTV to promote his *Late Registration* album, West said hip-hop was always about "speaking your mind and about breaking down barriers, but everyone in hip-hop discriminates against gay people." Inspired by the realization that his cousin is gay, West has called for the end of gay bashing in rap lyrics.

West couldn't have anticipated the fallout from such comments. Many of his fellow artists assumed he was gay for speaking out so forcefully. In response, West said that because of the antigay ignorance, hatred, and discrimination rampant in rap and hip-hop, he would never have made such comments if he himself was gay. Rather, he was sticking up for friends, family members, and fans. Given the level of hatred and violent lyrics directed at gay people in many rap lyrics, "I wouldn't have spoken on that if I was gay or if I was in the closet. I would have stayed so far

COURTING CONTROVERSY

away from it," he said to the *Manchester Evening News*.

Though West has sometimes made comments that he reconsidered later, he said that his outspoken nature is just the way he is, a quality instilled in him by his mother. He told the *Manchester Evening News*: "It's almost a character flaw in me to be emotional and honest like that. Sometimes it works out; sometimes it can backfire on you."

For Kanye West, with his over-the-top style, huge ego, supreme self-confidence, and larger-than-life persona, speaking his mind usually

Kanye West, among the most celebrated and successful artists in rap and hip-hop, continues to sell out concerts around the world, record his own music, and produce hits for other artists.

seems to work out just fine for him. His outspokenness, quick intelligence, verbal power, stubbornness, courage, and drive may occasionally land him in hot water. But they also make him the artist that he is, one who has struggled to the peak of hip-hop success and now towers triumphant.

39

TIMELINE

1977 June 8, Kanye West is born in Atlanta, Georgia.

2001 Jay-Z releases *The Blueprint*, featuring four songs produced by West; West goes on to produce hit songs by Ludacris and Alicia Keys.

2002 West appears as a guest on Jay-Z's 2002 album, *The Blueprint 2: The Gift & the Curse*; West raps for the first time on the album's single, "The Bounce"; Jay-Z offers West his own recording deal with Roc-A-Fella Records; West is involved in a serious car accident; he breaks his jaw in three places.

2004 West releases his debut album, *The College Dropout*; the album sells 441,000 copies in its first week.

2005 West, nominated for nine Grammy Awards, wins Best Rap Album and Best Rap Song for "Jesus Walks"; West releases his second album, *Late Registration*; it sells more than 860,000 copies in the first week it's released.

2006 West wins three of the eight Grammy Awards for which he is nominated: Best Rap Solo Performance for "Gold Digger," Best Rap Song for "Diamonds from Sierra Leone," and Best Rap Album for *Late Registration*.

2007 West releases his third album; after a rivalry with rapper 50 Cent, West's *Graduation* sells more than 957,000 copies in its first week; West's mother dies suddenly following surgery.

2008 West wins four awards at the fiftieth Annual Grammy Awards (he was nominated for eight Grammys), including Best Rap Album for *Graduation*; West launches his *Glow in the Dark* tour with concert dates throughout North America and Europe.

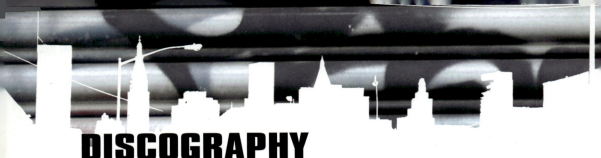

DISCOGRAPHY

2004   *The College Dropout* (Roc-A-Fella Records)
2005   *Late Registration* (Roc-A-Fella Records)
2007   *Graduation* (Roc-A-Fella Records)

GLOSSARY

Billboard 200   The Billboard 200 is a ranking of the two hundred highest-selling music long-playing (LP) albums and extended-play (EP) records (usually short records containing three of four songs) in the United States.

eight-bit sampler   A sampler is an electronic music instrument. Instead of generating sounds from scratch, a sampler starts with multiple recordings (or "samples") of different sounds, and then plays each sample back, often distorting or rearranging the previously recorded sounds to create something new and altered.

Grammy Awards   The Grammy Awards are presented annually by the National Academy of Recording Arts and Sciences of the United States to honor outstanding achievements in the record industry.

GLOSSARY

hip-hop Hip-hop is both a cultural movement and a type of music first developed in New York City in the 1970s by African Americans and Latinos.

levee A levee is a type of flood bank or stop bank that is a natural or artificial slope or wall, usually earthen and often paralleling the course of a river. Levees are designed to prevent flooding from swollen lakes and rivers or surging ocean tides.

materialism The belief that the highest values or objectives lie in material well-being, wealth, or owning an abundance of goods.

Nielsen SoundScan Nielsen SoundScan is an information system that tracks sales of music and music video products throughout the United States and Canada.

R & B Short for rhythm and blues, R & B is a popular music genre combining jazz, gospel, and blues influences. It was first performed by African American artists.

rap Rap, or rapping, is the rhythmic spoken delivery of rhymes and wordplay, one of the central elements of hip-hop music and culture.

record label A company that makes albums by signing artists and coordinating the production, manufacture, distribution, and promotion of sound recordings and music videos.

suburban Qualities of residential areas on the outskirts of a city or large town.

telemarketer A salesperson who invites prospective customers to buy products or services by phone.

FOR MORE INFORMATION

Kanye West Foundation
8560 West Sunset Boulevard, Suite #210
West Hollywood, CA 90069
Web site: http://www.kanyewestfoundation.org
The mission of the Kanye West Foundation is to help combat the severe dropout problem in U.S. high schools.

Recording Industry Association of America (RIAA)
1025 F Street NW, 10th Floor
Washington, DC 20004
(202) 775-0101
Web site: http://www.riaa.com
This trade group represents the U.S. recording industry.

WEB SITES

Due to the changing nature of Internet links, Rosen Publishing has developed an online list of Web sites related to the subject of this book. This site is updated regularly. Please use this link to access this list:

http://www.rosenlinks.com/lhhb/kawe

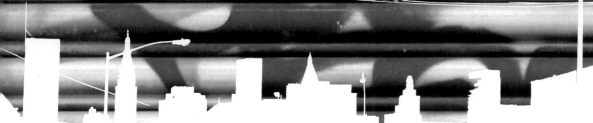

FOR FURTHER READING

Brown, Jake. *Kanye West in the Studio: Beats Down! Money Up! The Studio Years (2000–2006).* Phoenix, AZ: Colossus Books, 2006.

Miller, Uzoma O. *Kanye West: A Biography.* Westport, CT: Greenwood Publishing Group, 2008.

Simons, Rae. *Kanye West.* Broomall, PA: Mason Crest Publishers, 2007.

West, Donda. *Raising Kanye: Life Lessons from the Mother of a Hip-Hop Superstar.* New York, NY: Pocket Books, 2007.

BIBLIOGRAPHY

Christian, Margena A. "Dr. Donda West Tells How She Shaped Son to Be a Leader in 'Raising Kanye.'" *Jet*, May 14, 2007. Retrieved May 7, 2008 (http://findarticles.com/p/articles/mi_m1355/is_19_111/ai_n19206336).

Mar, Alex. "Kanye West Blows Up." *Rolling Stone*, September 7, 2005. Retrieved May 9, 2008 (http://www.rollingstone.com/news/story/7606082/kanye_west_blows_up).

McAlley, John. "Entertainer of the Year: Kanye West." *Spin*, December 20, 2007. Retrieved May 5, 2008 (http://www.spin.com/articles/entertainer-year-kanye-west-0).

Montgomery, James. "Kanye West Loses It Again, Says He'll 'Never Return To MTV': Report." MTV.com, September 10, 2007. Retrieved June 5, 2008 (http://www.mtv.com/news/articles/1569313/20070910/west_kanye.jhtml).

Ogunnaike, Lola. "Kanye West World." *Rolling Stone*, January 25, 2006. Retrieved May 5, 2008 (http://www.rollingstone.com/news/story/9183008/kanye_west_world).

Ogunnaike, Lola. "Kanye West's Mother a Model of Support." CNN.com, November 12, 2007. Retrieved April 22, 2008 (http://www.cnn.com/2007/SHOWBIZ/Music/11/12/west.mother/index.html).

Ryan, Gary. "Kanye's Winter Return." *Manchester Evening News*, September 14, 2007. Retrieved June 15, 2008 (http://www.manchestereveningnews.co.uk/entertainment/music/rock_and_pop/s/1013712_kanyes_winter_return).

Tyrangiel, Josh. "Why You Can't Ignore Kanye." *Time*, August 21, 2005. Retrieved May 7, 2008 (http://www.time.com/time/magazine/article/0,9171,1096499,00.html).

Vibe. The Vibe History of Hip-Hop. New York, NY: Three Rivers Press, 1999.

Vozick-Levinson, Simon. "Jay-Z's Brotherly Love." *Entertainment Weekly*, September 18, 2007. Retrieved May 7, 2008 (http://www.ew.com/ew/article/0,,20057568,00.html).

INDEX

C

College Dropout, The, 4, 21–24
Common, 4, 12, 24, 27

D

Dash, Damon, 7, 12, 20, 24

F

Foxx, Jamie, 21, 22, 26

G

Graduation, 4, 27–30
Grammy Awards, 20, 21, 24, 25, 30, 32, 38

J

Jay-Z, 4, 6, 7–8, 9, 12, 15–16, 21, 22, 24, 29

K

Kanye West Foundation, 36–37
Keys, Alicia, 4, 16
Kweli, Talib, 21, 24

L

Late Registration, 4, 26–27, 38
Ludacris, 16, 24

R

Roc-A-Fella Records, 4, 6, 7, 12, 14, 15, 16, 19, 20

S

Sigel, Beanie, 6, 9, 12

T

Twista, 21, 27

W

West, Donda, 5, 8–9, 13–14, 27, 36–38
West, Kanye
   awards won, 21, 24–25, 27, 30
   in car accident, 4, 19–21
   and controversy, 5, 31–36
   on homophobia, 38–39
   middle-class upbringing, 4, 8–9, 12–14, 19, 21, 23
   and mother's death, 5, 37–38
   musical influences, 9–12, 22
   as producer, 4–5, 6, 13–16, 18, 19, 22, 27, 30
   as rapper, 4–5, 6–7, 13–14, 16, 18–24, 26–39
   rivalry with 50 Cent, 5, 27–29

47

ABOUT THE AUTHOR

Laura La Bella is a writer living in Rochester, New York. She has eclectic taste in music, with an album collection spanning heavy metal, jazz, rap, hip-hop, pop, country, and classical. Among her favorite hip-hop artists are Run-D.M.C. and Kanye West.

PHOTO CREDITS

Cover Kevin Mazur/National Football League/Getty Images; p. 1 Stephen Lovekin/WireImage/Getty Images; p. 7 Johnny Nunez/WireImage/Getty Images; p. 10 Vince Bucci/Getty Images; p. 11 Jean-Marc Giboux/Liaison/Getty Images; p. 13 Tim Klein/Getty Images; pp. 17, 37 Frank Micelotta/Getty Images; p. 20 Kevin Winter/Getty Images; p. 22 Tim Mosenfelder/Getty Images; p. 24 Steve Granitz/WireImage/Getty Images; p. 26 Peter Kramer/Getty Images; pp. 28, 30 Brad Barket/Getty Images; pp. 32, 39 Dave Hogan/Getty Images.

Designer: Thomas Forget; Photo Researcher: Amy Feinberg